To my dear friend Glen

— Artie

2010

To my dear friend Glen

RESTAURANTS BY DESIGN

RESTAURANTS BY DESIGN

JOHN RIORDAN

COLLINS | DESIGN

An Imprint of HarperCollins*Publishers*

HarperCollins books may be purchased for educational, business, or sales promotional use.
For information, please write: Special Markets Department, HarperCollins Publishers Inc.,
10 East 53rd Street, New York, NY 10022.

First Edition

First published in 2006 by:
Collins Design
An Imprint of HarperCollins*Publishers*
10 East 53rd Street
New York, NY 10022
Tel: (212) 207-7000
Fax: (212) 207-7654
collinsdesign@harpercollins.com
www.harpercollins.com

Distributed throughout the world by:
HarperCollins*Publishers*
10 East 53rd Street
New York, NY 10022
Fax: (212) 207-7654

Art direction & Design by: Packaged by:
Agnieszka Stachowicz   GRAYSON PUBLISHING
                                     1250 28th Street NW
                                     Washington, DC 20007

Library of Congress Cataloging-in-Publication Data

Riordan, John.
  Restaurants by design / John Riordan.-- 1st ed.
      p. cm.
  ISBN-13: 978-0-06-089346-0 (hardcover)
  ISBN-10: 0-06-089346-X (hardcover)
  1. Restaurants--Decoration. 2. Interior decoration--History--21st century. I. Title.
  NK2195.R4T78 2006
  725'.71090511--dc22

                              2005034921

Printed in China
First Printing, 2006
Full title page: Nobu 57, Photography : SCOTT FRANCES

CONTENTS

FOREWORD

From their humble origins more than 300 years ago as places to feed weary travelers, contemporary restaurants have become places of high theater that feed not just the appetite but the soul as well.

Recent history has witnessed the emergence of an increasingly educated audience for these theaters. Entire networks, with small armies of superstar chefs, are devoted to entertaining an increasingly discriminating populace on how to properly prepare and enjoy food. Restaurants have evolved in kind, employing some of the most talented and recognized architectural and culinary specialists to insure this new culture is satisfied.

This book focuses on twenty-one contemporary restaurants that provide the guest with a cohesive design experience. Projects included illustrate places that are the product of designers working closely with the owner, chef, and sometimes other designers (graphic, clothing, etc.), and display an attention to detail rarely experienced. These are restaurants where the space, staff, service, and cuisine all reinforce the larger design concept—all conspiring to insure the diner will not leave disappointed.

LEFT: Dine among champagne-like glass bubbles at Mix, Las Vegas.
RIGHT: The flexible high-tech kitchen at Alinea

ARCHITECT Rugo/Raff Architect

INTERIOR Tom Stringer, Inc.

LOCATION Chicago, Illinois

PHOTOGRAPHER Charlie Mayer, Laura G. Kastner

Alinea

Through a play of light, shadow, and innovative perspective, Alinea becomes a black-box theater for Chef Grant Achatz's innovative cuisine.

Tom Stringer Interiors and architects Rugo/Raff have created a dining stage that complements Achatz's concepts for cuisine. The sequence of spaces within the restaurant are designed to at first disorient the guests from a typical dining experience, and then slowly reorient them. This sequence begins the moment they enter through the inconspicuous door off of Chicago's North Halsted Street.

Guests walk down a long hallway toward what appears to be a dead end, marked by a pulsating sculpture by designer Martin Kastner. Nearing the sculpture, stainless steel, sensor-activated doors part, allowing the guest into the "box."

Here, diners find a restaurant filled with rich fabrics, natural woods, and soft light. The dining rooms are small, ranging from sixteen to twenty-five seats per room. In each room, the use of plush fabrics and lighting create a private dining experience.

Custom wood dining tables are unadorned, providing a blank canvas for the chef's creations. Chairs were custom designed for

maximum comfort, since guests may be seated for up to six hours during the the typical twenty-five course meal.

An impressive blackened-metal and glass staircase leads to the upper level, visually connecting the two with its transparency. A white curtain acts as a translucent screen that breaks up the space into intimate areas. Flowers are changed daily, based on the season and the mood the chef wishes to create. The LED lighting system is also adjusted with the season.

Because of the experimental nature of his menu, Chef Achatz needed an unusual kitchen. In addition to the standard items in a commercial kitchen, Achatz needed induction heaters, a centrifuge, industrial blenders.

The plating and silverware change with each course. Chef Achatz worked with Czech-born jewelry and furniture designer Martin Kastner to develop a series of serviceware that would best complement the intricate and unusual presentations of the food. Diners have the choice of either ordering the fifteen or twenty-five course menus.

SECOND FLOOR PLAN

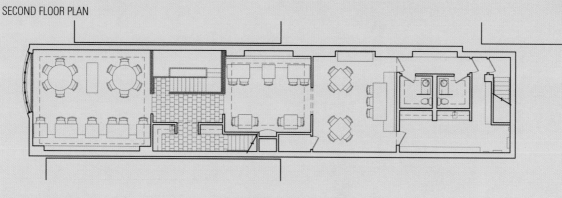

FIRST FLOOR PLAN

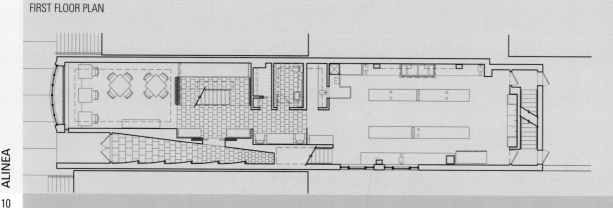

PREVIOUS PAGE: View of kitchen from entry
ABOVE: Blackened-steel and glass staircase
from downstairs entry to upstairs dining rooms
RIGHT: The main entry hall disorients guest
by means of a forced perspective.

ABOVE: Alinea's beautifully
presented turbot
FAR LEFT: A private dining room with
custom wood service station
LEFT: Matsutake

LEFT: Chef Achatz insists that the tables remain free of plating and stemware to dispel any preconceived notions of what the night's meal will be.

BELOW LEFT: Use of flowers and LED lighting change the mood and appearance of a room.

RIGHT: A pork belly dish mounted atop special plating hardware called the "squid"

ARCHITECT Lewis Tsurumaki Lewis

LOCATION New York, New York

PHOTOGRAPHER Michael Moran

Tides

All that the proprietors Steven Yee and Alan Leung approached Lewis Tsurumaki Lewis (LTL) with for the concept of a new restaurant was a small space on Manhattan's Lower East Side, a modest budget, and a passion to provide a menu with fresh seafood. What they got in return was a twenty-four-seat restaurant whose synthesis of material and space transports diners to the very source of their food.

The 420-square-foot former deli, is as tall as it is wide. To make the most of this space LTL decided to limit the material palette and modify the ceiling to create a better proportion within the space.

After blocking out the essential elements of the design, such as the bathroom, dining area, and kitchen, LTL determined that there was little room left for making a "large move." Drawing on their experience with similar small spaces, they decided to it was best to focus on a single ordinary material, manipulating it in various applications to transcend its conceived use. For Tides, they chose bamboo.

The scope of their use of this material is evident from the street front. At the entrance, bamboo snakes up a banquette and wall, one side peeling away to reveal custom recessed lighting. The other side is flanked with intimate built-in booths of bamboo strips lit by custom lighting fixtures.

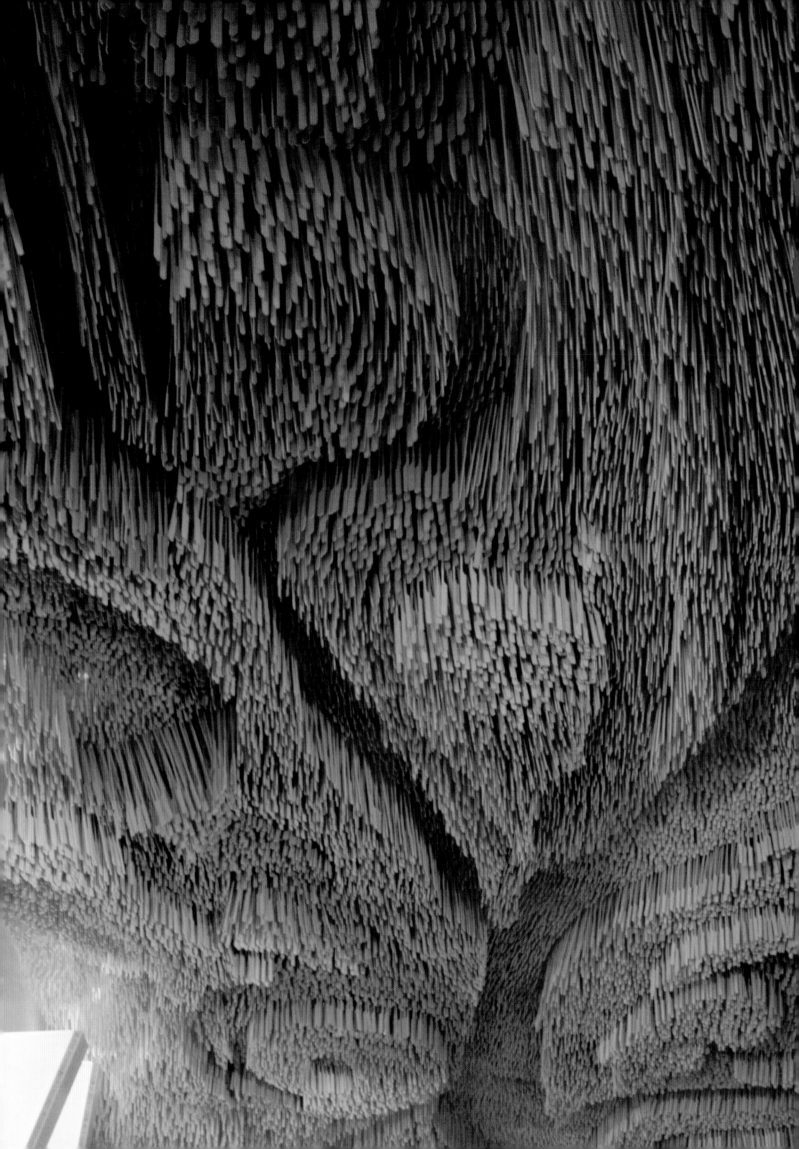

Even the ceiling is bamboo, a still life of sea grass, composed of more than 120,000 bamboo skewers. "We cornered the Eastern Coast market on bamboo skewers for a while," David Lewis said. Because of the artistic importance of the ceiling to the overall design, LTL's staff spent weeks working through dozens of prototypes to find the perfect combination of skewer, ceiling tile, and undulation. "Regular ceiling tiles would fall apart if you stuck this much into them," Lewis said. The architects found the perfect combination, and these tiles were then assembled in the office's shop (skewer by skewer) and hung in panels on site. The areas above the booths had to be painstakingly placed by hand in situ. They were able to back-light the composition, giving life to the material and space.

Since the idea of freshness played so heavily into the original concept of the design, the kitchen is connected to the dining space by a custom ice slide, designed to display fresh seafood. From the kitchen, Chef Judy Seto serves a mainly seafood menu that changes seasonally. The small but focused wine list changes with the food, so the two will always be perfectly paired.

CONCEPTUAL RENDERING

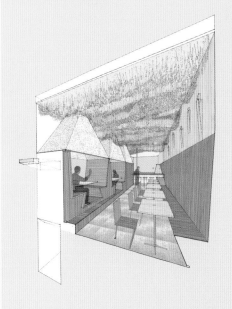

FLOOR PLAN

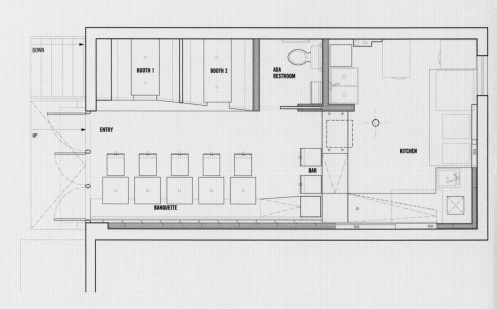

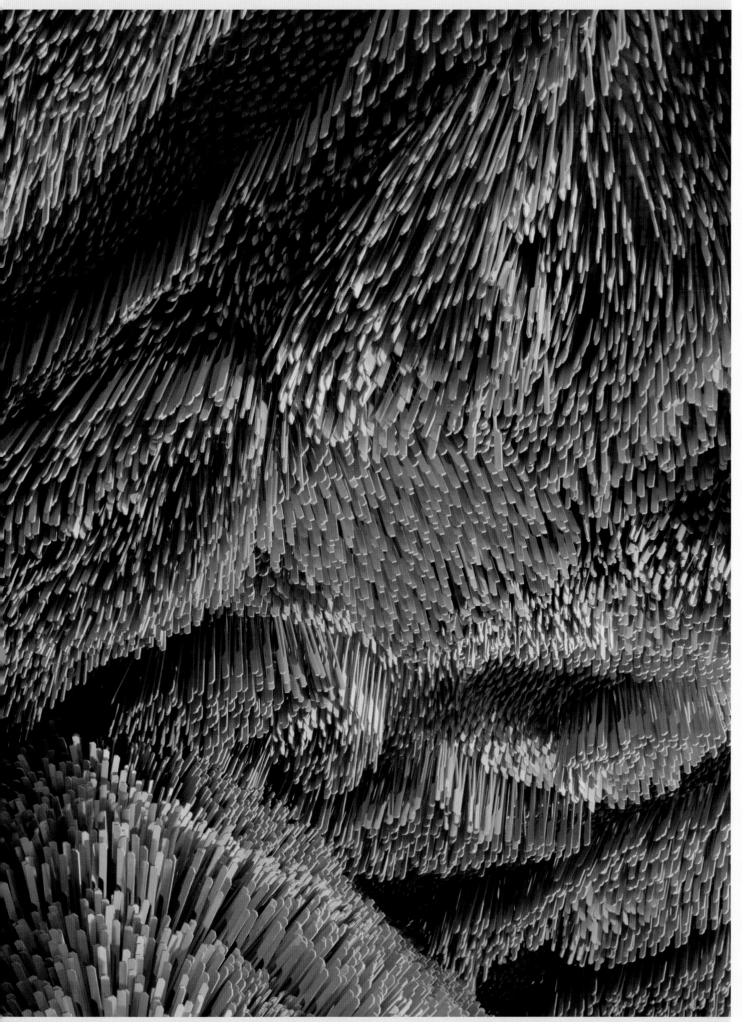

ABOVE: A custom door-pull adorns the inscribed storefront facade.
LEFT: Detail of custom LTL light fixture that is in each of the eating booths
RIGHT: Sea grass grows down from ceiling integrating one bamboo element to the next.

LEFT: Tides version of the French classic bouillabaisse
BELOW LEFT: Freshly seared scallops upon a bed of pumpkin puree, from the fall menu
RIGHT: An ice slide emerges from the kitchen area and is used to display fresh shellfish.

ARCHITECT Yabu Pushelberg
LOCATION Las Vegas, Nevada
PHOTOGRAPHER David M. Joseph

Shibuya

Taking its name and inspiration from a famous shopping and entertainment district in West Tokyo, Shibuya embraces modern and traditional design elements to create a perfect environment for Chef Eiji Takase to serve his innovative food.

The 7,000-square-foot L-shaped space is located in the MGM Grand hotel. The program called for a variety of Japanese dining experiences, including a sushi bar, a main dining room, a hibachi bar, and private dining rooms.

The journey begins when diners are greeted by the large barcode-like striped windows that separate the restaurant from the main hotel space. Guests are greeted at a handmade cherrywood maitre d' stand.

The sushi bar is the dominant design feature of the restaurant. A 50-foot-wide video wall is an allusion to the neon signs populating the restaurant's namesake district, as well as Las Vegas. It is made of fragmented glass cubes back-lit by dozens of televisions, chosen by the architects instead of newer LED technology because they are more cost-effective and because they provide a warmer light, more suitable for dining.

The sushi bar is flanked by two dining rooms. Yabu Pushelberg decided to use handcrafted elements to separate and define these

spaces. Screens of bent wood define the space and give a feeling of warmth and intimacy. Custom-made stacked-wood lanterns are dispersed thoughout the rooms.

To one side of the restaurant is the sake cellar, offering one of the largest collections in the United States. Located near the rear of the space is the dramatic Teppan room, surrounded with a back-lit wood screen. Each of the five hibachi tables is nestled under a pink stainless steel hood.

PREVIOUS PAGE: Custom wood screens activate the walls behind the teppanyaki table.
LEFT: Shibuya's lighted bar behind a glass screen, made to look like a barcode
RIGHT: The bar's light show is an homage to the lighted signs of the restaurant's namesake district in Tokyo.
BELOW RIGHT: Striking uplit glass walls lead to a custom host stand made from a single tree trunk.

FLOOR PLAN

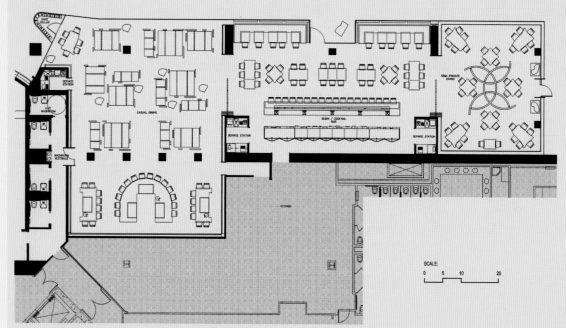

SCALE:
0   5   10   20

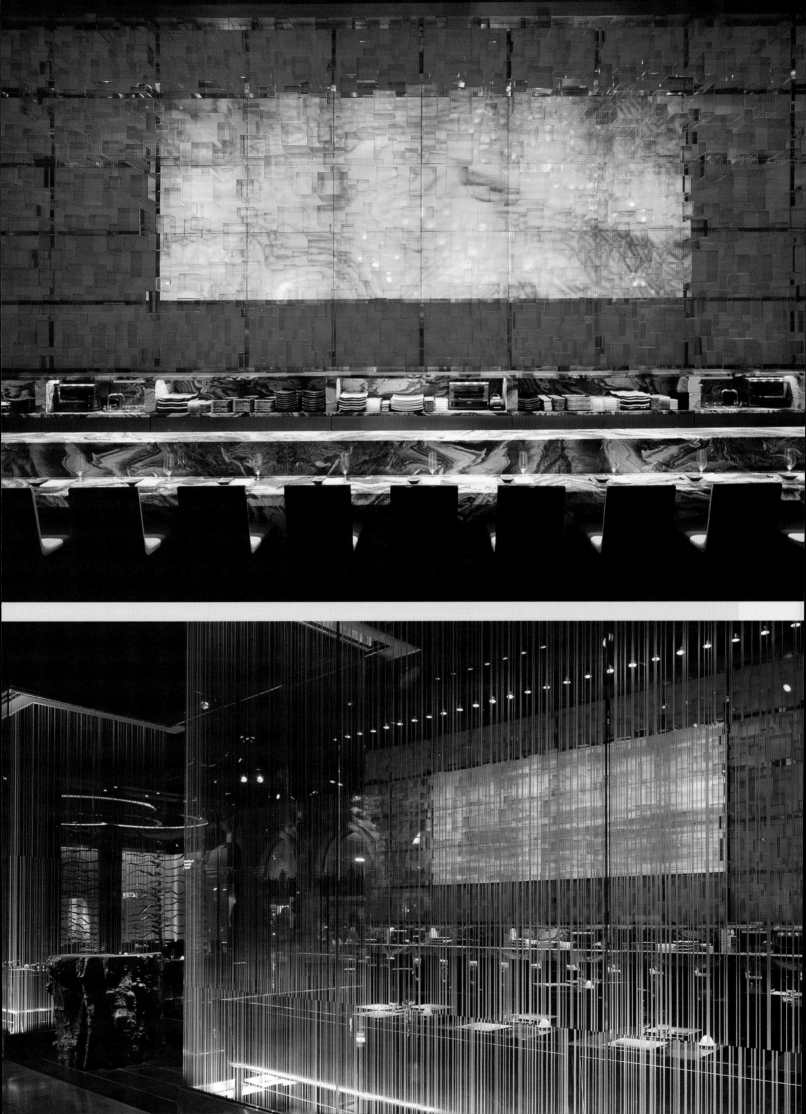

LEFT: The manmade stone sushi bar
dominates the entry area.
ABOVE: Tucked in one corner of the
restaurant is one of the largest selections
of sake in the United States.

ABOVE: Large vine-like screens drop from the ceiling, creating a visual stopping place for an otherwise enormous space.

ABOVE RIGHT: Soft pink stainless steel hoods hover over the restaurant's four teppanyaki tables.

FOLLOWING PAGE: The private dining area is defined by custom wood screens.

ARCHITECT Patrick Jouin

LOCATION Las Vegas, Nevada

PHOTOGRAPHER Eric Laignel, Thomas Duval

Mix

When the Mandalay Bay Resort Group wanted to create a world-class restaurant high above Las Vegas that would rival the restaurants of other culinary stars on the Strip, they chose the restaurateur Alain Ducasse and his longtime collaborator and designer, Patrick Jouin. The result is Mix Las Vegas, a 25,000-square-foot, 600-seat wonderland of space, material, and food perched 64 stories above the Strip in THEhotel at Mandalay Bay.

The program called for a 300-seat dining room and a 250- seat bar with additional tables on a heated terrace outside. With the luxury of space and volume, Jouin separated dining room and bar by a common kitchen. Guest access the restaurant via two glass elevators. Arriving at the 64th floor, diners pass through a low and narrow black portal designed to accentuate the enormous volume of the main dining room.

Dominating the dining room is Jouin's impressive chandelier of hand-blown glass bubbles. Some 15,000 separate bubbles make up this piece, which took more than two months to install. Beneath the chandelier is a sea of white tables and custom-designed chairs and banquettes.

The private dining room hovers above the main dining room, and is reached via a curved staircase, leading to a "silver cloud"—a paster and silverleaf platform. Once here, diners find themselves surrounded by Jouin's impressive chandelier.

Flanking either side of the dining room is an impressive glassed-in wine locker and the centralized kitchen, open to view. Guests dine on specially designed plates.

On the other side of the kitchen, the bar exudes a darker, more intimate feeling with a lower ceiling and a rich material palette. Banquettes of dark leather snake thorough the space. An organic structure above the main bar both dominates the room and conceals the VIP lounge above that can be accessed only through a door located behind the bar. A champagne bar enjoys panoramic views of the city.

PREVIOUS PAGE: The custom handblown-glass chandelier fills the large main dining room.
LEFT: A dark-wood entry heightens the effect of entering into the large, light-filled dining room.
RIGHT: Detail of handblown-glass ball that makes up one of thousands needed for the entire chandelier
FAR RIGHT: VIP dining area above the main dining room

FLOOR PLAN

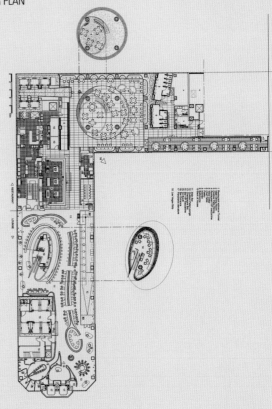

BELOW LEFT: Lobster salad
BELOW RIGHT: Champagne bar commands
a view of the Las Vegas skyline
BELOW AND OPPOSITE: The entry and
corridor to the bedroom as seen from the
living area
FOLLOWING PAGE: The main bar, with the
VIP section hidden above

ARCHITECT Yabu Pushelberg

LOCATION Minneapolis, Minnesota

PHOTOGRAPHER David M. Joseph, Mark LaFavor

Cosmos

Housed in Graves 601 hotel in downtown Minneapolis, Yabu Pushelberg's restaurant, bar, and club, with a sense of timeless modernity, communicated by his use of warm materials and clean, simple forms.

In the dining room and lounge, walls are lined in horizontal grained wood, seating fabrics are wool, and downlighting is accentuated by custom floor lanterns—all adding to the overall cozy effect. The lounge is covered floor to ceiling in red upholstery and serves as the core of the restaurant.

In contrast, the bar utilizes a palate of stone, back-lit glass, and leather fabrics to reinforce a sense of coolness. The bar-top is lit from underneath using the state of the art LED technology that casts a million-color-spectrum light off the surrounding white materials, changing the feel of the room several times over the course of the night. Custom artworks personalize each space.

Chef Seth Daugherty's cuisine draws upon seasonal ingredients from surrounding farms as well as from fishmongers in New York City. The menu changes monthly.

FLOOR PLAN

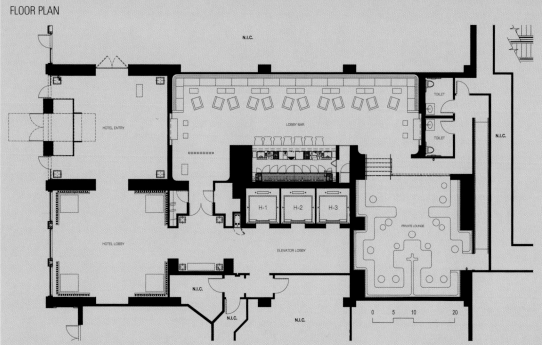

PREVIOUS PAGE: Wood paneling and warm lighting create an intimate dining nook.

ABOVE: Host desk surrounded by custom glass work

ABOVE RIGHT: Main dining room

RIGHT: Maine lobster tail over freshly grilled summer vegetables

COSMOS

44

ABOVE: View of bar from lobby
LEFT: The use of warm materials makes the lounge area a place to relax.
RIGHT: Custom artwork exemplifies the high level of craftsmanship evident in the construction of the restaurant.

LEFT: A long black-leather banquette dominates
the lounge area of the club.
ABOVE: A deep red palette creates the almost
womb-like atmosphere of the club area.

ARCHITECT Top Pot, Inc.

LOCATION Seattle, Washington

PHOTOGRAPHER Spike Mafford, Joe Shlichta

Top Pot

When Mark and Mike Klebeck and partner Joel Radin started selling handmade doughnuts in a small coffee shop on Seattle's Capitol Hill, they had no idea it would lead to a local doughnut empire with stylish headquarters in the middle of downtown Seattle.

Faced with growing sales of their artisan doughnuts and an undersized kitchen, the Klebeck brothers found a 1950s art storage warehouse on Seattle's Fifth Avenue that met their size and aesthetic requirements and began the renovation.

The result is steel-framed glass facade with a double height space featuring a lower main level and an upper mezzanine intended for overflow and private functions. A post–World War II motif was used for the decor. Visitors are greeted at the entrance by a custom neon sign that bears the Top Pot logo with a 1950s buckaroo.

Custom terrazzo adorns both floors, complemented by woodwork, tables, and reclaimed library chairs—all in a honey finish. Customers order from the large display case and espresso area adorned with a back-lit menu printed in postwar-inspired cursive fonts.

Metal workers who are longtime friends of the Klebeck brothers created the Moderne-style interior metalwork—from the metal screen work to the hand and guard rails at the stairs.

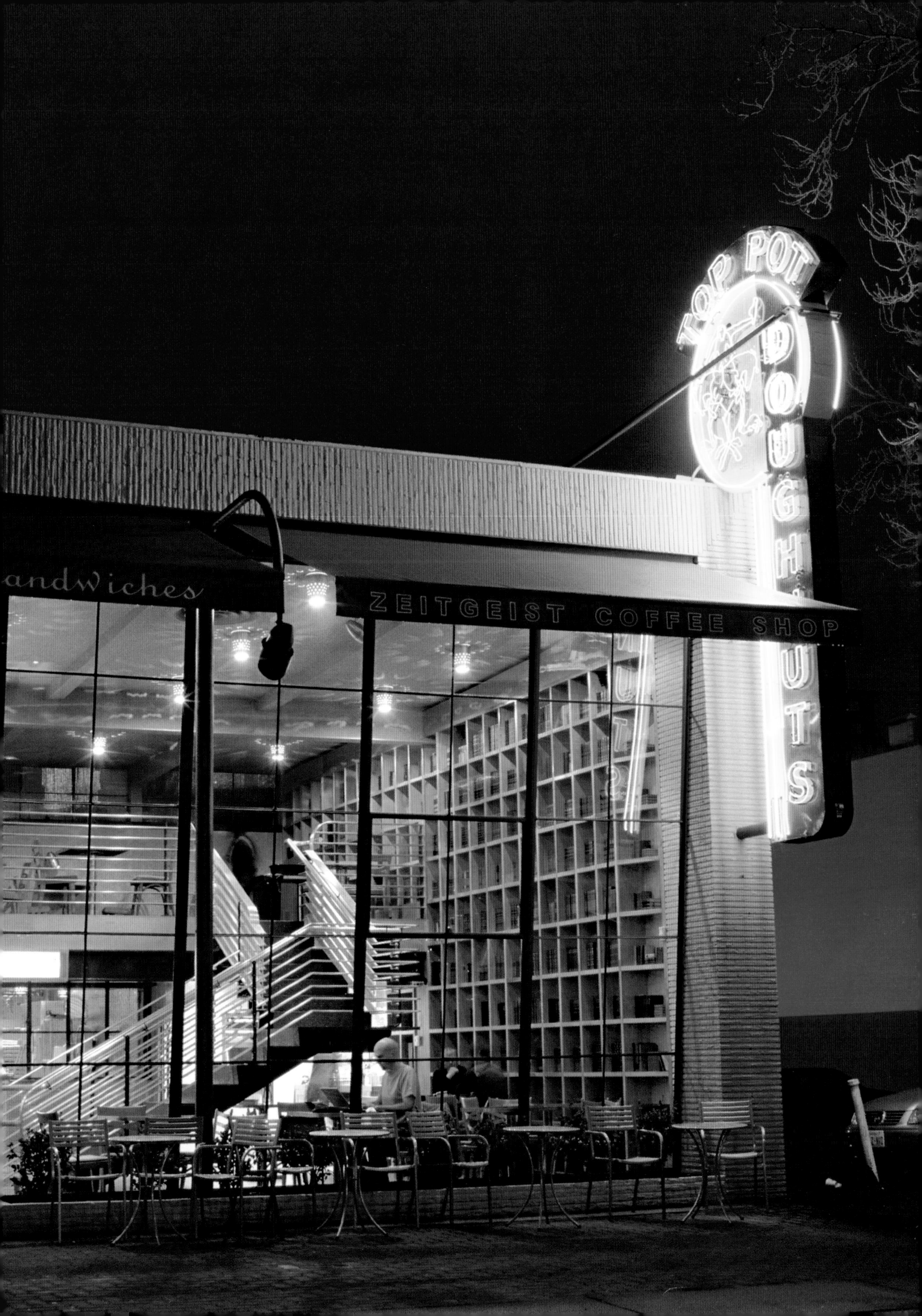
TOP POT
DOUGHNUTS
andwiches
ZEITGEIST COFFEE SHOP

More than half the floor space is dedicated to the kitchen which can be seen through a viewing window at the main level. The brothers found a line of stoneware similar to that of dinnerware in the postwar period. Each dish and saucer has the Top Pot logo, printed in a blue reminiscent of the period.

FLOOR PLAN

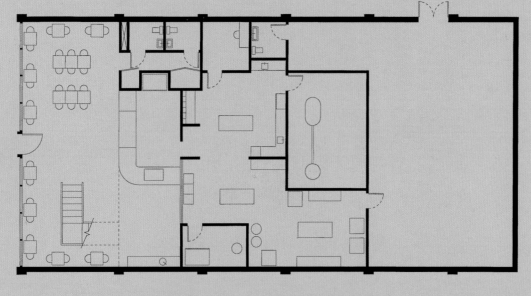

PREVIOUS PAGE: The entry facade

TOP LEFT: Custom aluminum work by Matt
Shoudy informed by a post–World War II
style adorns the new stairway.

ABOVE: Blonde-stained custom woodwork
acts as a warm contrast to the cold terrazzo
floor and aluminum work. Venetian plaster
wall finishes are by Tina Randolph.

LEFT: A mezzanine was added to original
floor plan to create seating and an area for
private events.
ABOVE: Custom woodwork, period inspired
typeface on the menus, and lucky horseshoes
greet visiting doughnut fanatics. Hand-
painted signage is by Russ Rasmussen.

ABOVE: Top Pot's custom dinnerware, showcasing their famous doughnuts and roasted coffee

LEFT: All coffee beans (drip and espresso) are roasted in-house on the Top Pot coffee roaster shown here.

RIGHT: The original steel-framed glass facade was kept to open up the space to the often scarce Seattle sunshine.

ARCHITECT Adamstein and Dimetriou
LOCATION Washington, District of Columbia
PHOTOGRAPHER Fredde Lieberman

Inde Bleu

Inde Bleu is a place in the nation's capital where French and Indian cuisine collide. It is a bar, a club, and a restaurant, including a private dining room and a chef's table. The Washington design firm of Adamstein and Dimetriou helped select this downtown spot as the best in the city for tracking the type of clientele the owners wanted. It is located only minutes from the national mall and White House in one of the city's emerging areas for gourmet dining and entertainment.

Because the clientele of each of the distinctive areas of the restaurant can differ, Adamstein and Dimetriou located the bar/club portion far from the dining area. Diners are ushered up the glass stairs to the main dining room. The bar and club are on the first floor.

Rich white silk curtains, custom silk-upholstered chairs, and mahogany greet arriving guests upstairs, where the tables are set with white tablecloths and plated with Indian-informed chargers. The private dining room is a deep red in keeping with the Indian-inspired dercor of the restaurant. Red silk upholstery and a roaring fireplace alludes to the cuisine and space's spicy origin.

To add a bit of theater to the space, Adamstein and Dimetriou placed a "diner's table" at the entrance to the kitchen. Instead of being a stationary table, at the mercy of the volume and activity of the kitchen, Inde Bleu's unique table is part of the action, functioning as a private space within itself. The entire banquette turns via pulleys and a "wheel" located outside of the booth. The entrance of the banquette turns toward the kitchen, putting the kitchen front a center from the vantage point of the table.

Downstairs, guest are greeted by a long white marble bar and red-clad DJ station that leads to the club in back. The rich warm fabrics and upholstery give a feeling of intimacy to the bar area. Custom leather booths define smaller spaces.

Diners may chose from a Chef Vikram Garg's prix fixe menu, or navigate the fusion cuisine using the restaurant's interactive menu. Each of the items reflects the fine balance of the different, but compatible, worlds of France and India.

FIRST FLOOR

SECOND FLOOR

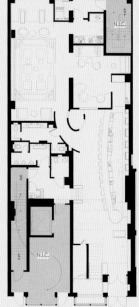

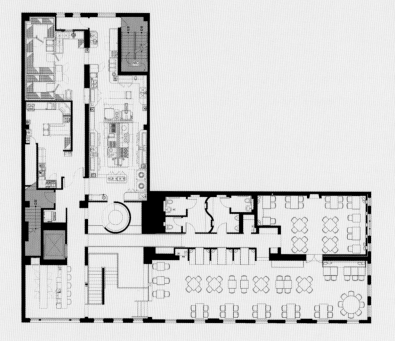

PREVIOUS PAGE: Inde Bleu's red dining room may be separated from the main space for private dining.

ABOVE: Chef's table in "open" position

RIGHT: Chef's table in "closed" position, allowing diners to look directly into the kitchen

ABOVE: Chef Garg's French-Indian inspired sea bass

RIGHT: The use of color and material reinforce the French-inspired decor in the more formal of Inde Bleu's dining rooms.

FAR LEFT: The curve of the marble bar at the entrance invites the eye to move to the club beyond.

ABOVE: Extensive use of custom furniture enhances the club area.

LEFT: An oval window provides a view of the naturally lit bar beyond.

ARCHITECT Skylab Design

LOCATION Portland, Oregon

PHOTOGRAPHER Basil Childers, Steve Cridland

Doug Fir

Using historic allusion, regionalism, play, and innovation, Portland's Skylab Studio converted an old hotel restaurant space into a convergence of new and old.

Located in Portland's formerly seedy East Burnside neighborhood, Doug Fir began as an idea for just a nightclub. Skylab's Jeff Kovel, and local music industry legends Mike Quinn and John Palmer, quickly realized the greater potential for the former restaurant space, and a restaurant, bar, and year-round outdoor lounge were added to the program.

Upon entering the space, Kovel provides guests with the option of continuing either into the main lobby, flanked by a dining room and bar, or moving downstairs to the nightclub. This configuration enables each section to operate independently and allows the complex to say open seven days a week, twenty-one hours a day.

In designing the new space, Kovel took his cues from the existing structure. Beneath dropped ceilings he found a unscathed waffle slab that would later become the nightclub's ceiling and pristine bent-glue-lam wood beams that supported the roof. These elements were combined by Kovel to achieve a log cabin–informed regionalism.

Upon entering the lobby, guests are greeted at a fur-covered podium. A piece of exploded and reassembled old growth timber makes up the bar that runs from the lounge area into the dining area. Custom

shoehorn-shaped banquettes dominate the dining space. Light enters through the original storefront windows. At night, candlelight and exposed-bulb ceiling fixtures accentuate the warmth from the surrounding wood decor .

Large stacked-timber walls line virtually every room, making the log cabin reference explicit. Kovel left the original fir beams exposed and completed the ceiling with wood slats.

The lounge area opposite the dining area is complete with a gas fireplace, leather upholstered, built-in seating, and log remnants for footrests. A wilderness mural adorns one wall, while deer antlers and glass game trophies can be found elsewhere. The heavy timber walls are broken by a piece of glass at seat level that visually connects this space with the outdoor seating area. The outdoor lounge, too, has a gas-fueled campfire and ample seating.

In the club below, a bar made from stacks of reclaimed lumber is lit from below by the luminescent floor. A large mirror around the perimeter breaks the timber wall, allowing people to see one other without being seen.

The menu has simple fare, featuring ingredients from local organic farms.

STREET LEVEL

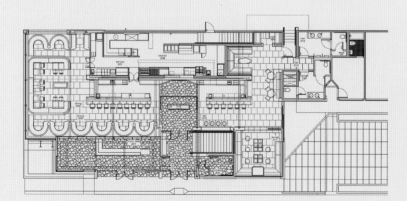

BASEMENT

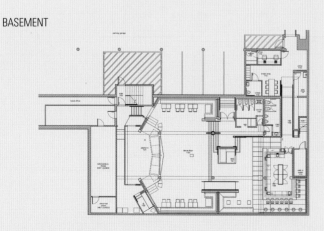

PREVIOUS PAGE: Doug Fir's future-past bar
TOP RIGHT: Street-level lounge with a view of the host area
RIGHT: Existing glu-lam beams preserved in main dining room

ABOVE LEFT: The interior glass fireplace illustrates a modern take on cabin vernacular.
ABOVE RIGHT: This stone pier acts as a screen and visual anchor to the lounge area.

LEFT: The exterior patio is equipped
for fireside chats.
ABOVE: Street elevation

LEFT: The entry canopy leads to fur-covered host stand.
ABOVE: Glass breaks in log walls allow for screened views into music venue within.
RIGHT: The Doug Fir uniform is a play on Forest Service unifroms.

ARCHITECT Barbara Berry

LOCATION San Francisco, California

PHOTOGRAPHER Eric Laignel, John Ormond

Michael Mina

Driven by tone and subtle gestures this designer/chef team quickly came to a united vision: to create a dining environment like the food—"simple, elegant, fresh and not about fashion." Michael Mina is located in the historic St. Francis Hotel in downtown San Francisco, and it is Berry's subtle, deliberate gestures that add up to a grand experience visually as well as gastronomically.

The experience begins upon entering the hotel lobby, which Berry opened the restaurant directly onto via a grand marble staircase. At the top of the stairs a greeting station displays a subtle bronze "MM" logo. Inside, the grand dining area is flanked by a long black-and-white veined marble bar at one end. Large multipane windows flood the room with light. Grand columns and intricate wood wall paneling from the hotel's original 1904 construction complete the design. Berry chose a subtle palette of grays and browns to establish the correct "canvas" on which to depict Mina's cuisine.

Through a series of perspective sketches, Berry designed the furniture in the dining room so as to break the space down into more intimate components. Each table is simply laid with a candle, a setting of stemware, and a service plate made of mother of pearl.

Uniforms are by local designer Dean Hutchinson and napkins have been custom-dyed, to Berry's specification, a "San Francisco sea fog." Special plating was designed to best present Mina's creations. This extraordinary serving had to have special Plexiglas and rubber bus tubs to protect it after use.

Chef Mina's menu represents the culmination of the culinary philosophy and techniques he has been refining since starting at San Francisco's well regarded Aqua more than eleven years ago. He calls his menu "complex simplicity," using seasonal flavors in up to six different ways to make an overall dish and taste experience.

PREVIOUS PAGE: Barbara Berry's design engages the lobby of the St. Francis Hotel with use of a dramatic staircase.
RIGHT: Luxurious materials and subtle changes in color complete palatte bar area.

FLOOR PLAN

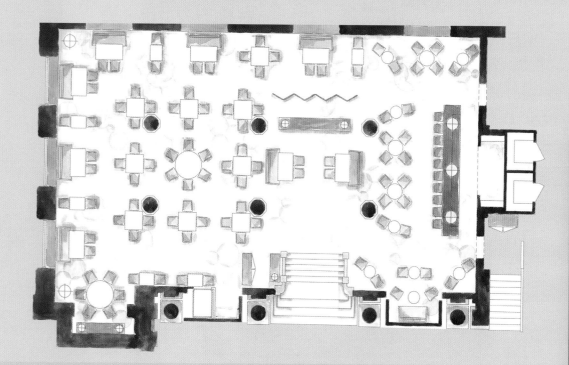

ABOVE: Pacific prawns three-ways
BELOW: Pork six-ways
ABOVE RIGHT: Sketch of dining room
RIGHT: Main dining room

A series of sketches illustrating Berry's design methods for chairs and seating (shown at right).

ARCHITECT Bentel & Bentel

LOCATION New York, New York

PHOTOGRAPHER Eduard Hueber, Quentin Bacon

The Modern

In their latest restaurant, The Modern, Bentel & Bentel uses a limited modernist palette of materials, an abundance of natural light, and efficient space design to create a fitting gallery for Chef Calders Kreuther's Alsatian-inspired cuisine.

The restaurant has a bar and café area and two formal dining areas. The restaurant has two entrances, one from the street and the other from within the museum via a passageway through an impressive display of the restaurant's large wine collection. This massive grid of bottles acts as a screen for the back of the bar, and provides small glimpses of the restaurant from between the wine bottles.

Entering the restaurant from either entrance, the bar and café dominate. Bentel & Bentel took full advantage of the low ceilings in this area to create a less formal and more intimate dining and social area. A long custom black leather bench acts a border between bar and café. As if to create a window to the art world just next door, the mural, The Clearing, by the contemporary German artist Thomas Demand, hangs on the museum side of the café. A frosted glass screen brings in light from

the Abby Aldrich Rockefeller Sculpture Garden, while protecting the privacy of the formal, double-height dining area behind it. A custom horseshoe-shaped banquette lines the perimeter to add warmth to an otherwise stark room and directs the diner's gaze to the sculpture garden beyond. A dining patio supplements the formal dining area, allowing guests to dine alfresco in the more temperate months.

PREVIOUS PAGE: Back-lit glass entry off of New York's 53rd Street
RIGHT: Artist Thomas Demand's lifesized photo of his own handmade leaves provides a portal to lounge and bar area.

FLOOR PLAN

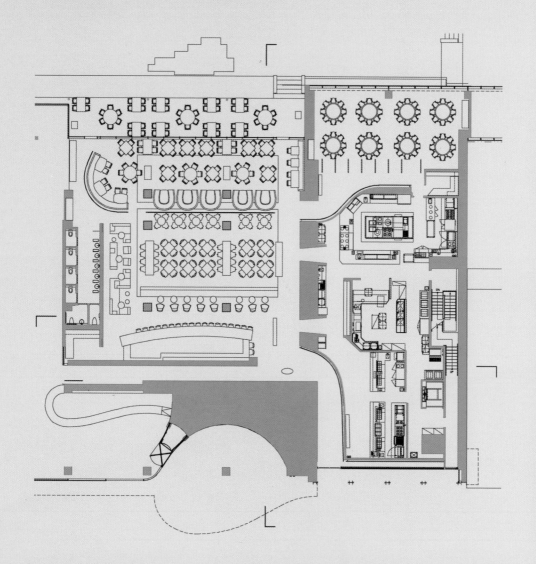

ABOVE: A custom bench separates bar from café area.

LEFT: The Modern's extensive wine collection is displayed in custom coolers that line entry from the museum.

RIGHT: The formal dining area takes full advantage of Taniguchi's new ,double-height curtain wall.

FAR LEFT: Door to exterior private patio allows for formal dining within the original sculpture garden.
ABOVE AND LEFT: The artfully designed food has found a perfect home.

ARCHITECT Lewis Tsurumaki Lewis

LOCATION New York, New York

PHOTOGRAPHER Michael Moran, Miso, Inc.

Xing

Architects Lewis Tsurumaki Lewis were asked by the clients to create a "modern interpretation of a Chinese restaurant without the kitsch", all on a very modest budget. The space is deep and narrow, and LTL wanted to avoid isolating the back space from the front. Their solution was to connect the front and rear by overlapping the various functions of the restaurant and creating a "stitch" that would unite them all. Each area of the restaurant, from the entry to the bar to the dining area in the rear is identified by its own distinctive material and color palette.

Diners enter through a bamboo portal. The stitch begins here and continues to the dark red formal dining area in the rear, eventually ending at the bathrooms. The stitch is constructed of 10,000 linear feet of thick jade green acrylic strips.The bathroom doors are acrylic with custom metal hardware.

Natural wood is used in most of the central dining area. Red velvet fabric walls dominate the rear dining area, while dark slate floors run throughout the restaurant.

Because the restaurant serves lunch and diner, the area nearest the door marks the more informal and public space. The bar area utilizes durable materials of slate and acrylic, gradating to the center area of hardy bamboo. The plush back dining room was designed to create intimacy.

PREVIOUS PAGE: Jade green resin "stitch" uniting front bar area with back area.
ABOVE: A custom-made, glass door pull marks the entrance.
RIGHT: Bamboo was used for the front dining area where the resin "stitch" is visible overhead.

FLOOR PLAN

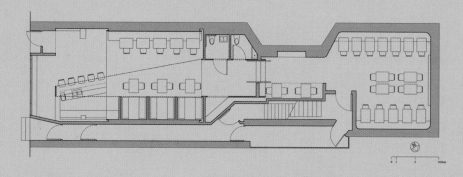

COMPUTER MODEL

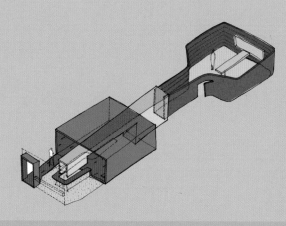

ABOVE: Resin seam feature turns into bar top.
ABOVE RIGHT: Red felt panels that line
dining room are mounted on Velcro and are
removable for ease of cleaning.

ABOVE: A view to the front of the restaurant from the rear dining area
LEFT: Crab Rangoon
RIGHT: The acrylic stitch connects the front bar to the rear dining area.

ARCHITECT Yabu Pushelberg

LOCATION Tokyo, Japan

PHOTOGRAPHER Nacāsa & partners Inc.

Golden Tongue

The genesis of this high-end restaurant and bar in the Ebisu district of Tokyo was to provide the neighborhood with a place that respected the Japanese manner of dining while exuding elegance and refinement. To stay true to its original conception, Yabu Pushelberg used a palette of luxurious materials, customized artisan elements by locals, and deft manipulation of space. Changes in elevation within the restaurant are used to distinguish the main dining room, the private dining room, and the bar.

Diners are first greeted by a striking double-height dining area that is accentuated by art installations. Stainless-steel screens surround tables, and metal screens made of blackened steel and polycarbonate by artist Hirotoshi Sawada minimize the size of the space by creating limited sight lines and by drawing light from the light-wells above. Diners in each corner of the main dining room are elevated on a platform and separated by one of the metal screens.

The bar is located just off the dining area and is made of an artificial material called "rocky mist." The designers were able to use large slabs, giving the impression expansiveness and refinement not

found in tiled applications of stone. Behind the bar is a commanding, two-story, back-lit wine and liquor storage tower.

Dark wood floors surround the "rocky-mist" stone that further defines the main dining area. To improve the existing curved staircase, the designer clad the structure in granite. The VIP area is located on the mezzanine level to best take advantage of the lower ceilings, giving the space a more intimate feeling. The handrails are custom made from a gold metal. A custom metal screen, built to evoke memories of rain, provides privacy for this area.

PREVIOUS PAGE: VIP dining area
RIGHT: A dramatic staircase ascends to private dining area above.

FLOOR PLAN

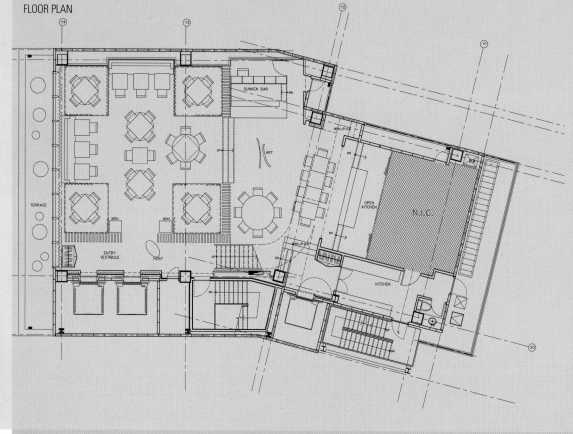

ABOVE: Metal curtains surround dining tables.
RIGHT: The stone of the bar cascades to floor plane of main dining area.

ABOVE: Bar dining area
LEFT: The ceiling plane mimics cross pattern below.
RIGHT: The dramatic double-height main dining room

ARCHITECT Kester, Inc.

LOCATION San Francisco, California

PHOTOGRAPHER David Wakley, Scott Kester

Frisson

Through the innovative use of space, textures, light, and transparency, designer Scott Kester creates a place where San Francisco diners can begin and end the night.

The concept for dining came from managing partner Andrew McCormick's experiences in Barcelona, Spain. While there he witnessed a form of nightlife called "la marcha," in which families and young people alike enjoy the city and public dining from sunset to early the next morning. McCormick wanted the new restaurant to transplant this idea to San Francisco.

Kester's strategy was to avoid to any direct links to Spanish origins, and to create a space that in its essence was inviting, comfortable, and varied.

To make the most of the ambitious program and 5,000-square-foot space, it is divided into smaller, more intimate parts. The bar, the lounge, the main dining room, the back garden, the chef's table, and the plating kitchen all make up the ground level. Below, Kester located the prep kitchen, downstairs lounge, and shared restroom space.

The bar area is placed closest to the street. Use of dark leathers, low lighting and a DJ station draw in the casual diner. This space marks the start of the experience, the "La Marcha." Bar patrons get a controlled

view of the "Stage," the circular dining room that is the dominant design element. With its 25-foot-diameter ceiling and its custom bench seats, this area is the place to see and be seen. Mingling patrons and staff are forced to move around the area by a short wall with screens that allow for partial views of action. These screens, made of resin and fabric panels stacked in a Bertoia inspired pattern, create partial views of the bar and kitchen areas beyond.

A private dining room just off the main circle is designed for small private parties. Its strategic location allows for views into the kitchen and garden area. This room, which is outfitted in rich browns, has a custom wood table and chandelier.

The rear garden area provides a way for diners to be outside without having to mill around on the street. Designed to keep diners engaged in the interior environment and to provide an outside space for guests who want to smoke, Kestler uses small planters to break down the scale of the space. A lounge area is located downstairs.

To encourage guest to stay, Kestler manipulates the lighting to create different moods. Behind the perforated circular ceiling fixture lie long tubes of various colors of neon. The low and warm setting of the "sunset" changes the room, while allowing the patron to remain stationary. In symphonic connection with the lights, the live DJ plays music that will complement the change in setting. The lights are placed on a fifteen-minute timer that allows for a slow, almost imperceptible change from yellow to red, dusk to sunset.

PREVIOUS PAGE: Service set-up in dramatic circular main dining room
RIGHT: The edge of dining area defines traffic patterns between dining and bar areas.

FIRST FLOOR PLAN

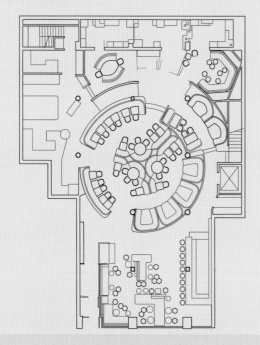

BASEMENT PLAN

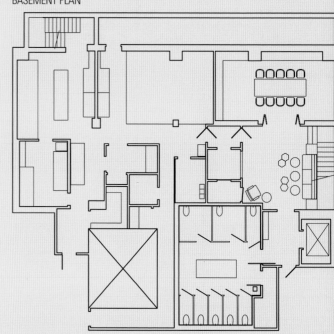

ABOVE: There is direct visual and audio
connection between areas through
custom screens.
LEFT: Detail of resin screen

RIGHT: Seared Dover sole over celery and
butter sauce
BELOW RIGHT: Roasted pork tenderloin
over faro beans

TOP LEFT: Private dining area
off of kitchen
LEFT: Private garden area
RIGHT: Main dining room looking
through bar to street

ARCHITECT Prast Hooft

LOCATION Amsterdam, The Netherlands

PHOTOGRAPHER Jeroen Musch, Willem Vandenberg

Harkema

Follow Nes Street north from Amsterdam's Dam Square you will find Brasserie Harkema subtly hidden amid the city's finer theaters. The designers were asked to renovate the original space and provide a bar, as well as main and private dining areas, in an old tobacco warehouse. The concept was to maintain some relationship to its industrial origins, but make the space more modern, timeless, elegant, and cozy.

The designers delineated the functions through height, material and light. Entering though oversized wooden doors into the glass entry vestibule allows the diner a first glimpse of the space beyond. The bar, closest to the entry, is at the lowest level. Covered in wood and bathed in warm light from the space's attractive light fixtures. To maintain a visual connection to the rest of the space while maintaining the autonomy of the bar, the designers installed a curtain of fine metal chains.

Diners step up into the main dining room, which during the lunch service is filled with natural light from the north-facing skylights above. Some walls from the original space were eliminated to accentuate the openness of the space. The dining room is filled with custom tables and benches from Prast Hooft. A floor to ceiling punchcard-like wine rack flanks one side of the room, while a multicolored wall activates the wall opposite. The custom stairs of bent blackened-steel lead to the private

dining area, complete with a service bar. From here, diners can passively join those below, while being served from the kitchen by a private stairway. The lower level features sleek bathrooms, and a small lounge for private phone conversations.

The space's warehouse attributes (large open volume), demanded that the renovation confront the difficulties of acoustics, while maintaining the sleek aesthetic. The substantive wall of wine near the kitchen utilizes a sound-absorbing material, while the wall opposite is made of wooden acoustical panels, painted in 100 different hues (the color of which is inscribed on each strip). To maintain the industrial origins of the space, the designers kept some of the original objects and materials, such as the wood floor, skylights, and metal radiators.

The menu is decidedly French-influenced, with nods to local dining preferences (delicious frites and cerlerac salad). The wine list is small, but focused on properly complementing the food. The list includes a comprehensive chart that rates the compatability of each wine with a corresponding menu option (one being ill-suited and five being ideal).

PREVIOUS PAGE: Natural light floods main dining room.
RIGHT: Delicate glass entry belies the restaurant's industrial origins.
BELOW: The metal curtain creates a striking separation between the bar and dining area.

FLOOR PLAN

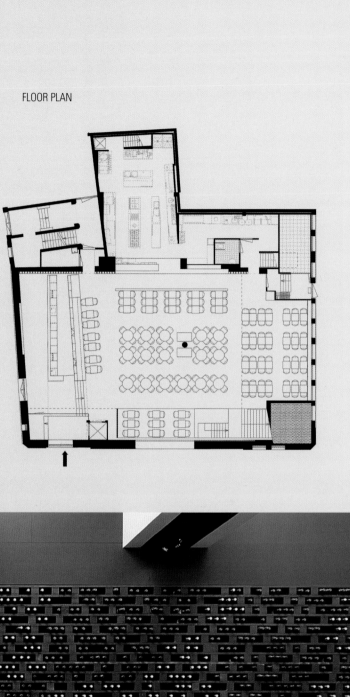

LEFT: A warm bar area greets
diners upon entry.
RIGHT: A dramatic bent metal
sheet staircase

ABOVE: Ante–dining room defined by
dropped ceiling caused by mezzanine above
LEFT: View from private dining area to main
floor below

RIGHT: Salmon tartar with chives and
citrus-butter sauce
BELOW: A wine wall built of sound-
absorbing material acts as damper for
main dining area.

ARCHITECT Atelier Hitoshi Abe

LOCATION Sedai City, Japan

PHOTOGRAPHER Shinkenchiku-sha, Daici Ano, Hayato Ikegami

Aoba-Tei

Hitoshi Abe's design provides an Eden for this invitation-only restaurant in Sedai City, Japan. From the Japanese for "leafy place", Abe drew inspiration from the famous Zelkova street trees to solve the 2,300-square-foot space's biggest problem—it is split unequally between floors. Abe wanted to connect entry and dining areas using one design gesture. He first considered changing the skin of the building.

Abe wanted to soften the cityscape by projecting patterns of street trees onto the curtain wall. When the owner's lease would not allow for such construction, Abe turned inward, bringing the treescape to the dining experience by creating a technically complicated yet poetic skin of perforated metal. The digitized motif was laid out on a virtual single sheet of thin steel and then bent in a volume that would eventually define the restaurant space. To make the complicated mammoth shell from thin metal sheets, a computerized shipbuilding factory located hundreds of miles away was employed. The single piece then had to be cut into smaller pieces for transportation and reassembly.

These perforated panels are separated from the structural wall and back-lit to achieve a dappled sunlight effect. Light for evening dining at the tables is supplemented by standard incandescent downlights.

To reinforce the guests' connection with nature, Abe had them enter through the intimate, off-street lobby filled with seasonal greenery. An LED-lit staircase leads from the entry to the lobby area.

As the main dining room slowly emerges, guests may dine in the bar area or in the more formal space near the curtain wall. The bar is set in the traditional dining configurations, where diners can more easily interact with the restaurant owner and host.

FIRST FLOOR PLAN

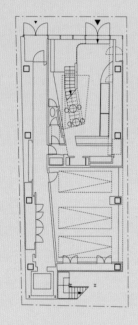

SECOND FLOOR PLAN

PREVIOUS PAGE: Diners ascend to the sun-dappled upper floor via a lighted stairway.
ABOVE: The extent of bent metal skin on interior is evident from street elevation.
RIGHT: Diagram demonstrating the virtual bending of metal skin
FOLLOWING PAGE: View of the second floor dining area

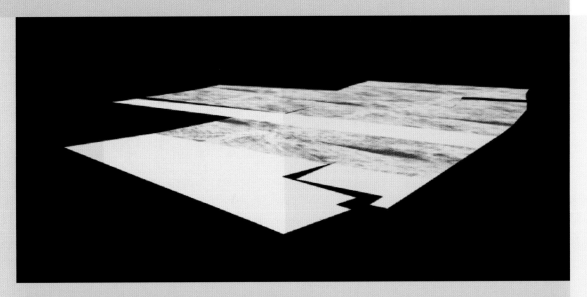

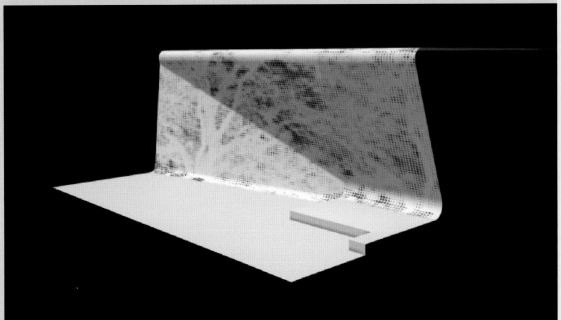

ABOVE: Custom walnut bar area were
patrons can converse with chef and host
RIGHT: A delicate quiche placed upon
a custom plate with Zelkova-inspired
flower motif

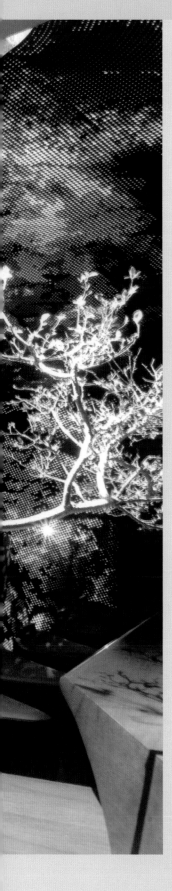

LEFT: View of lobby area with planting bed
and dramatic stairway that separates from
the skin of the interior
ABOVE: The leaf pattern of Zelkova tree
outside was used to provide perforated
pattern shown.

ARCHITECT Matali Crasset

LOCATION Paris, France

PHOTOGRAPHER Patrick Gries, Chez Pim

Vēgētable

Located in the 9th Arrondissement of Paris is one of the city's more famous and busy department stores, Le Printemps. Occasionally the store organizes events around a theme, setting up temporary exhibition space. For only a month, in late Spring of 2005, the store opened Parentheses Vēgētale ("vegetable parenthesis"), which marked the second such exhibition for the store, and a growing movement in Paris: "restaurant ephemere" or temporary restaurants.

These ephemeral restaurants are whimsical as well as temporary, with some becoming a restaurant within a restaurant.

For Parentheses Vegetale, Le Printemps tapped the talents of two of the most influential designers in France today, Matali Crasset and Chef Alan Passard, to create "Vegetable" (a pun in French conjoining the French equivalent of vegetable and table into one word) to celebrate Passard's influential vegetarian cooking and back-to-the-farm philosophy.

Matali, who is know for making complete, versatile, and playful environments, took to heart the whimsical and temporary nature of ephemere and Passard's statement in 2001 as he was permanently deleting red meat from his Michelin three-star menu. "Vegetables are so much more colorful, more perfumed. You can play with the harmony of colors, everything is luminous," Passard said to Freepress.

Once located on the fourth floor, the restaurant space was separated from the main store space by a temporary modular screen of green resin resembling ivy.

More hints of bright "vegetable" green snake through the table tops, as bent wood, rustic is used to create everything from coat racks, to chandeliers.

In reference to the vegetables being eaten, Crasset back-lit a wall of individually potted grass with fluorescent grow-lights, exposing the diners to the same beneficial light as their green counterparts.

To complete the allusion, custom plates were made with the motif of a dandelion—chosen for the ephemeral nature of its seed-flower, and the suggestion that Passard's near-religious devotion to the native soil and vegetables might spread.

Much of the affordable café menu and its ingredients were taken directly from a sister three-star restaurant, L'Arpege. The same vegetables placed on the TGV each morning from Passard's own garden outside of Paris make their way to both places. Much of the same staff were used as well, but were dressed down in Végétable street-garb.

PREVIOUS PAGE AND RIGHT: Detail of green resin screen
BELOW: Cane-covered chair design created by Crasset for the restaurant

FLOOR PLAN

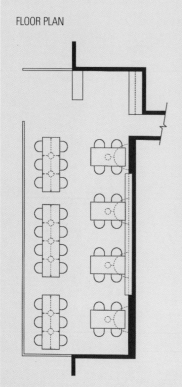

végétable

alain passard — matali crasset

ENTRÉES

Chaud froid d'œuf fermier
Sirop d'érable 8 euros

Velouté potager à la moutarde d'Orléans
Crème soufflée 9 euros

Aigre doux « Arlequin »
Navet au romarin 11 euros

Crème de champignons aux cacahuètes
4 épices 9 euros

Etuvée de petits pois au pamplemousse
Basilic 10 euros

PLATS

Gratin d'oignons doux des Cévennes
Poivre noir Sarawak 12 euros

Croque « légumes » au parmesan
Salade pastorale 15 euros

Ravioles maraîchères aux herbes fines
Consommé végétal 17 euros

Risotto « printanier »
Primeur du jardin 15 euros

Pousses d'épinard au sésame

végétable*

alain passard — matali crasset

BOISSONS

Champagne Billecart Salmon Brut
8 euros

Anjou Blanc « Clos des Treilles »
Nicolas Réau 5 euros

Château la Gordonne Rouge
Eric Verdier 7 euros

Eaux minérales 3 euros

Cafés 3 euros

Infusions et Thés 4 euros

Cocktails de fruits et légumes 4 euros

Sodas 4 euros

alain passard

est un chef viscéralement attaché à ses fourneaux
depuis 30 ans.
Tel un peintre impressionniste, il ne cesse à petites
tâches de chercher à rendre le meilleur du produit
avec pour souci de le respecter. Il se fait l'interprète
d'une saveur en privilégiant l'authenticité.
Préservant sa couleur, son essence, ses teintes, son
parfum de peau, il restitue la pureté du produit.

matali crasset

ABOVE: Passard's simplified three-star menu was designed by Crasset.

LEFT: Dandelion-motif plateware was also designed by Crasset and manufactured by Bernardaud.

BELOW LEFT: Chocolate cakes with lemongrass-infused crème anglaise

RIGHT: Bent-wood piping and detailing allude to temporary nature of construction.

LEFT: Passard's famous herb-filled ravioli in broth
BELOW LEFT: Strawberry dessert
RIGHT: Bent-wood chandeliers

ARCHITECT Bentel & Bentel
LOCATION New York, New York
PHOTOGRAPHER Eduard Hueber, Bill Bettencourt

Craft

Starting with the culinary concept of Chef Tom Colicchio's—preparing simple, soulful dishes centered around single ingredients—Bentel & Bentel changed an old clothing store into a feast for the eyes and a perfect complement to the food.

The design, like the culinary concept, is elegant yet unadorned. Materials are left exposed in their natural beauty. Elements of the store's original construction is often juxtaposed with the restaurant's newly crafted items

Original brick walls and terra-cotta-clad columns are left exposed, while new handmade features fill the space. The rich texture of leather panel–clad walls contrasts with the colder custom metal wine tower opposite. This wall of wine not only hides the route from the kitchen below but adds to the dramatic sweep of the space. The bartop is the actual worktable from the ironmonger's studio where the wine wall was created. Bentel & Bentel intentionally left this metal unfinished so that it would naturally patina with use, like the original material of the space.

Exposed light bulbs are arranged in organized clusters over custom cherrywood tables in the main dining room.

Bentel & Bentel manage to comfortably fit a dining area for 130, a kitchen up to the task, and a 3,500-bottle wine cellar into a 2,900-square-foot ground floor and 2,200-square-foot basement.

Diners order from a menu of "main dishes" and "sides" to "craft" their own meal. Each dish is meant to stand on its own, or be combined with any number of sides. A chef's tasting menu of more than twelve items is said to be the best way to experience the craft from the kitchen.

FLOOR PLAN

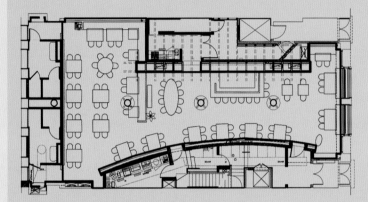

PREVIOUS PAGE: The original brick wall left exposed as archeological reference to original craft of space
RIGHT: Curved leather paneled wall hides bathroom and service areas from main dining area.
BELOW: Rows of original columns and custom lights visually break up deep space.

LEFT: Dramatic wine wall fills double-height space.

BELOW LEFT: Detail of leather panels exposes the craft needed to make them blend seamlessly.

RIGHT: Stainless steel mesh cradles each bottle, allowing for adequate air movement to properly cool wine.

BELOW RIGHT: Detail of custom metalwork of wine wall

LEFT: Lobster tail
BELOW LEFT: Rosemary encrusted beef
RIGHT: Bentel & Bentel preserved original storefront windows to make dramatic use of natural light.

ARCHITECT Asfour Guzy and Machado Silvetti Design

LOCATION Pocantico Hills, New York

PHOTOGRAPHER Michael Moran, Mora McEnvoy

Blue Hill

Blue Hill at Stone Barns and Stone Barns Center for Food and Agriculture provides a unique campus for diners to experience the entire farm-to-table concept its Manhattan namesake pioneered more than a decade ago.

The original Blue Hill in Manhattan had the culinary philosophy of providing fresh local and seasonal food in a way that allowed the diner to experience the essence of the food. This began with Dan Barber's earlier experience cooking for friends. Most of the food was purchased from Washington Square's famous local food purveyors. In 1985 he and his partners (Laureen Barber, and Chef Michael Anthony) opened Blue Hill.

The new Blue Hill at Stone Barns and Center are located in Pocantico Hills in New York's Hudson River Valley, only forty minutes by car, but a world away from the urban location of the original Blue Hill. The Stone Barns campus is a combination of a working restaurant, farm, and educational center.

David Rockefeller, a regular diner at their Manhattan establishment, agreed to donate the old farm buildings and 80 of the estate's 4,000 acres in memory of his late wife, Peggy, and her beliefs in stewardship of the land. The Barbers' idea was to draw on the year-round farming ideas of the Four Season Farm in Maine, adding a one-acre greenhouse to the already ambitious program.

The design concept for the campus was to utilize as much of the existing structure as possible, retaining the look of the original farm. New structures were kept to a minimum, and modified or expanded parts utilized a substantial amount of glass to obtain a light look. The large program called for a conference center, restaurant, farm, education center, greenhouse, café, and general support structures. Gardens are dispersed throughout the campus to reinforce the connection between cuisine and agriculture.

Diners and visitors to the education center approach via a long drive that passes through the first of these gardens. Two silos, modified to house a coat check room and waiting area, flank the entrance to the restaurant and the main convention space.

The old cow barn was modified to house the restaurant. The restaurant was to reflect the honesty of the food and dining space's origins. To prevent diners feeling like they were eating in a converted barn, Asfour Guzy finished the original space with neutral materials but only the "bones" are exposed to allude to the space's industrial past. Hand-troweled plaster offers a wonderful canvas to highlight the exposed wrought-iron metalwork that made up the barn's original roofing. Reclaimed pine floors complete the allusion to the old. The Blue Hill team hired a local artist to paint the Hudson Valley landscape mural at one end the main dining room. Laureen Barber, the design director, worked with longtime collaborator, Alexander. Together they created the "look" of the restaurant and learning center, using familiar and accessible iconography related to farm life. The printed materials are in keeping with the spirit of the venture with the use of eco-friendly, high-quality inks and papers.

The menu changes seasonally, but adheres to a prix fixe–type menu. Diners have the option of three to seven courses, the largest named "Farmer's Feast," offering a selection of whatever is freshest, often picked in the late morning.

PREVIOUS PAGE: One of many fields that supplies Blue Hill at Stone Barns with seasonal produce.
ABOVE RIGHT: View of campus from main drive
FAR RIGHT: Section through restaurant

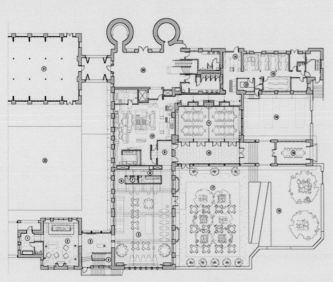

BLUE HILL AT STONE BARNS

1 ENTRY
2 BAR
3 RECEPTION
4 STAIR TO BATHROOMS
5 MAIN DINING ROOM
6 SOMMELIER
7 WINE ROOMS
8 SERVICE BAR & COFFEE
9 VESTIBULE
10 PRIVATE DINING FOYER
11 PRIVATE DINING
12 KITCHEN
13 CHEF'S OFFICE
14 KITCHEN ENTRANCE & RECEIVING
15 WALK-INS, STORAGE & LOCKERS
16 HERB GARDENS
17 OUTDOOR DINING
18 OUTDOOR PRIVATE DINING
19 GARDEN
20 EVENT SPACE ENTRY HALL
21 EVENT SPACE
22 STONE BARNS COURTYARD

NORTH

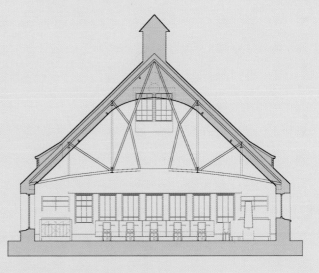

LEFT: Old grain silo stands guard over campus entrance.
BOTTOM LEFT: Main courtyard
RIGHT: Entrance to main courtyard from parking lot

ABOVE: Post-renovation of cow barn area
LEFT: Pre-renovation of cow barn
ABOVE RIGHT: Lecture space in the old barn
RIGHT: The waiting area is located in the old silo.

ABOVE: The large greenhouse is able to supply the restaurant with year-round supply of fresh produce.
LEFT: Farm fresh egg and asparagus
ABOVE RIGHT: A small courtyard houses an herb garden.
RIGHT: Site Plan

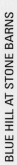

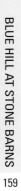

BLUE HILL AT STONE BARNS

ABOVE LEFT AND RIGHT: Main dining area
in metal rafters of old barn. The architect
tried to retain as much of original metalwork
as possible.
FOLLOWING PAGE: A view of the herb garden

ARCHITECT Hirsh Bedner

LOCATION Las Vegas, Nevada

PHOTOGRAPHER Bill Milne for Bill Milne Studio

Okada

Okada is one of the restaurant jewels in the Wynn Las Vegas resort, which offers one-stop shopping for gourmet diners. Longtime design partners with Wynn, the L.A. firm of Hirsh Bender was charged with a design that would reflect Chef Takashi Yagihashi's culinary vision. The designers used architectural details to make specific allusions to tradition while using materials and colors to reflect a more contemporary vision.

Hirsh Bedner felt the most important aspect of tradition was to emphasize the Japanese connection to the landscape. Making full use of its location, Wynn and Hirsh Bender created a literal oasis with the Japanese garden. Regardless from the time of day or season, the connection to the outside garden is made evident from the moment the diner walks through the custom iron gates. Accordion glass doors can retract to open the connection to this garden from the private and main dining rooms. The serenity portrayed beyond is meant to draw guests in from the harried casino environment.

The hostess desk is intentionally subtle, allowing guests to fully engage with the space, surveying the options for dining laid out before

making a choice. Diners wishing a more Western experience move forward to the main dining room. Overhead are full timbers connected by traditional leather-strapped joinery.

The Teppanyaki Room consists of six Robatayaki grills and hoods that are hidden behind wooden canopies. Here the use of light metal and folded metal sheets reinforce the contemporary feel, while floor to ceiling windows allow diners to view the manicured garden outside.

VIPs may dine at a single table placed in the middle of the garden. Because of the extremes in temperature in a desert environment, heaters and misters are hidden nearby.

Large sake barrels made by local artisans adorn the end of the sushi bar. To complement Chef Yagihashi's menu, Okada provides one of the largest sake collections in the United States. A sake sommelier is on hand to guide you thorough the 300-plus brand selection.

FLOOR PLAN

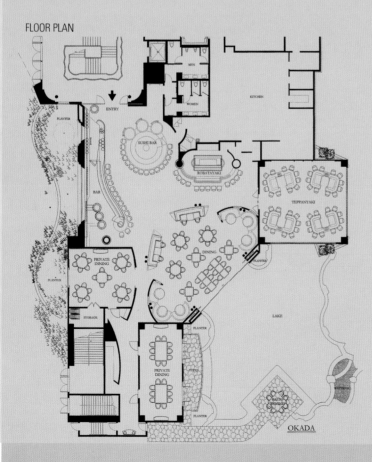

PREVIOUS PAGE: Handmade sake barrels act as an anchor to the large sushi bar.
RIGHT: Restaurant space opens up from entrance, allowing the diner to move to the middle of the space before deciding where to dine.

LEFT: Okada's play on the bento box
BELOW LEFT: One of many vegetable-meat combinations available from the restaurant's Robatayaki grills
RIGHT: Direct visual connection to exterior garden and private dining area is unusual for Las Vegas dining.
OPPOSITE: The entry and corridor to the bedroom as seen from the living area

LEFT: Playful tempura
BELOW LEFT: Tuna tartar with a
horseradish sauce
RIGHT: Main dining room retains
connection to striking garden beyond.

ARCHITECT Studio Gaia
LOCATION Mexico City, Mexico
PHOTOGRAPHER Jamie Navarro

Solea

Solea brings the soul of Mexico city to an international venue in the W Hotel's latest addition to its burgeoning string of high-design hotels. To do this Studio Gaia of New York used a warm color palette, transparency, and indigenous materials.

Diners are offered the first glimpse of the restaurant from the lobby. A twelve-seat private dining room is suspended between the main dining room. The room is filled with plush fabrics in warm hues offset by a double-height stone wall.

Guests ascend the stairs from the light-filled main lobby to the darker main dining room and bar. Chocolate-colored walls, ebony-stained wood floors, and warm red light fill the room.

Private dining banquettes made of an indigenous Mexican stone called Cantera Paloma and red glass add privacy to the open dining area.

The bar area, serving chocolate-flavored fare, is located near the rear of the space. Custom white leather chairs, lamps, and tables add contrast to the darker, more linear environment left behind.

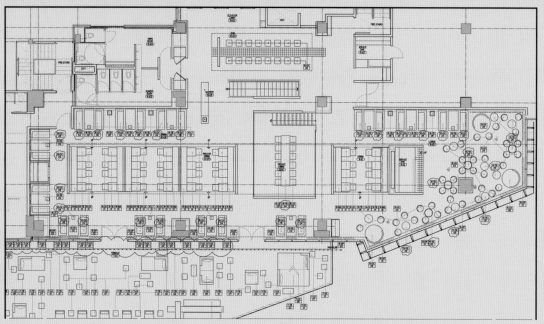

PREVIOUS PAGE: Native stone and red glass panels define the more private dining booths of Solea's main dining room.

ABOVE: Bar area

RIGHT: Native stone wall creates a visual connection of the lighter lobby below to darker interiors of bar above.

ABOVE: The lounge is fitted with custom
white ,leather furniture.
RIGHT: A private dining area bridges the
lobby and restaurant levels.

FAR LEFT: The lounge has a visual
connection to streetscape.
ABOVE: Dining booths
LEFT: View from booths through
red glass

ARCHITECT Rockwell Group

LOCATION New York, New York

PHOTOGRAPHER Scott Frances, Gwen Shlichta

Nobu 57

To design the twelfth location in the now burgeoning Nobu chain, David Rockwell returned to his roots with the genesis of the Nobu empire.

In the original and still popular Nobu space in downtown Manhattan, the Rockwell Group drew inspiration from Nobu Matsuhisa's cooking and his cultural roots in the Japanese countryside. The latest design for Nobu draws on the same inspiration but clarifies the architectural language to that of a traditional Japanese fishing village.

For this location in midtown Manhattan, Rockwell was given the shell of an old ski store to fill with the newest expression of Nobu. Rockwell broke up this double-height cavernous space into a bar and small dining area at ground, elevating the main dining space to the mezzanine level.

To transport the visitor from the busy Manhattan streetscape to a peaceful Japanese fishing village, Rockwell first created a portal at the street edge. Diners enter through a space with stacked walnut timbers that focus their attention onto the aquatic-inspired world ahead.

The rough-hewn walnut bar looks like a piece of driftwood, and the walls and columns are sheathed in timberstrand shingles resembling those on Japanese Timberstrand houses. Soaring sake barrels, caged in traditionally jointed walnut, project vertically from the bar and accentuate the volume of the first-floor space. At the ceiling, large waves made of reed mats allude to fishing nets suspended in the ocean. Thousands of

silvery abalone shells in chandelier format draw attention back to the waved terrazzo floor and reinforce the feeling you have walked off the street and onto a seabed in Nobu's native Japan. And as you pass the back-lit onyx maitre d' desk and ascend the stairs to the main dinning room, you approach the ocean's surface.

The main dining room is enveloped on three sides by an undulating banquette. On the fourth side, which turns into the sushi bar, Rockwell installed a terrazzo embedded with bamboo cross-sections. The effect is that of a Japanese manga version of bubbles, created perhaps by the metaphoric waves passing just overhead.

The hierarchy of the restaurant culminates in a beautifully apportioned private dining room surrounded in peen-hammered copper to mimic a pebbled beach. An intricate ceiling panel made of thousands of sea urchin tentacles hangs from the center of the room.

Chef Nobu Matsuhisa remains as innovative as ever with a few modifications to the original menu. Many of his ingenious flavor combinations remain (creamy spicy sauce with tempura), but with new variations on the original, such as king crab lightly fried in tempura batter garnished with jalapeño in a delicious pool of ponzu sauce.

FIRST FLOOR PLAN

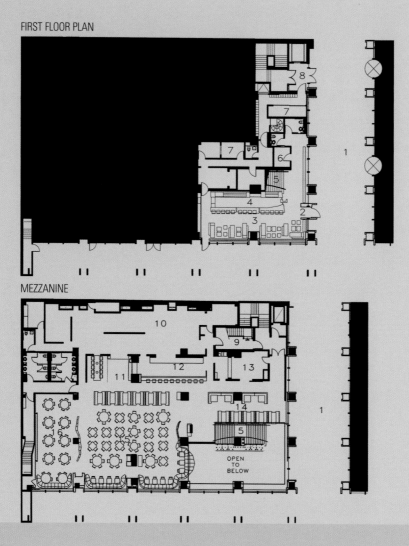

MEZZANINE

PREVIOUS PAGE: Small window in private dining area allows for visual connection to sushi bar beyond.
RIGHT: Restaurant as seen from midtown street front
BELOW RIGHT: Custom onyx host stand
BELOW FAR RIGHT: Walnut portal transports diners from streetscape to host stand.

FAR LEFT: More than 20,000 abalone shells were needed to complete the shell chandeliers.

LEFT: A desert consisting of carmel and lavender with komomo apricot foam and cocoa mikado

ABOVE: Upstairs dining area

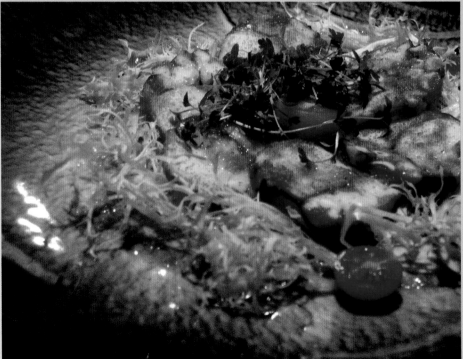

ABOVE: Upper dining area, surrounded by custom resin panels

ABOVE RIGHT: Sushi bar

LEFT: Octopus carpaccio with frisee and jalapeno vinegarette

RIGHT: Nobu's signature dish of black cod cured in miso and garnished with haji kan

FOLLOWING PAGES: Sea urchin–spined ceiling in main dining area

DIRECTORY

Alinea
1723 North Halsted
Chicago, Il 60614
Phone: (312) 867-0110
www.alinearestaurant.com
Interior:
Tom Stringer, Inc.
62 West Heron St
Chicago, Il 60610
Phone: (312) 664-0644
Architect:
Rugo/Raff Ltd Architects
20 West Hubbard Street
Chicago, Il 60610-6254
Phone: (312) 464-0222

Tides
102 Norfolk St,
New York, NY 10002
Phone: (212) 254-8855
Designer:
LTL Architects
147 Essex Street
New York, NY 10002
Phone: (212) 505-5955
Fax: (212) 505-1648
www.ltlarchitects.com

Shibuya
MGM Grand Hotel
3799 Las Vegas Blvd South
Las Vegas, NV 89101
Phone: (702) 891-3001
www.mgmmirage.com
Designer:
Yabu Pushelberg
55 Booth Avenue
Toronto, Ontario M4M 2M3
Phone: (416) 778-9779
Fax: (416) 778-9747

Mix Las Vegas
THE Hotel at Mandalay Bay
3950 Las Vegas Blvd South
Las Vegas, NV 89119
Phone: (702) 632-9500
www.thehotelatmandalaybay.com
Designer:
Patrick Jouin
8, Passafe de la Vonne Graine
75011 Paris, France
Phone: 22 (0) 1 552 88920
www.partrickjouin.com

Cosmos Restaurant
Graves 601 Hotel
601 1st Ave North,
Minneapolis, MN 55403
Phone: (612) 312-1168
www.cosmosrestaurant.com
Designer:
Yabu Pushelburg
55 Booth Avenue
Toronto, Ontario M4M 2M3 Canada
Phone: (416) 778-9779
Fax: (416) 778-9747

Top Pot
2124 5th Avenue
Seattle, WA 98121
Phone: (206) 728-1966
www.toppotdoughnuts.com
Designer:
Top Pot, Inc.
2124 5th Avenue Seattle, WA 98121
Phone: (206) 728-1966
Fax: (206) 728-1956

Inde Bleu
707 G Street, North West
Washington, DC 20001
Phone: (202) 333-BLEU
www.bleu.com
Designer:
Adamstein and Demetriou
3247 Q Street North West, 2nd Floor
Washington, DC 20007
Phone: (202) 333-9038
www.ad-architects.com

Végétable (closed June 2005)
64 bd Haussmann
75009 Paris, France
Phone: 33 (0)1 42 82 50 00
Designer:
Matali Crasset
26 Rue du Buisson
Saint Louis, F-75010 Paris, France
Phone: 33 (0)1 42 40 99 89
www.matalicrasset.com

Craft
3 East 19th Street
New York, NY 10003
Phone: (212) 780-0880
www.craftrestaurant.com
Designer:
Bentel and Bentel
22 Buckram Road
Locust Valley, NY 11560
Phone: (516) 676-2880
www.bentelandbentel.com

Blue Hill at Stone Barns
630 Bedford Road
Pocantico Hills, NY 10591
Phone: (914) 366-9600
www.bluehillstonebarns.com
Designer:
Ashfor Guzy Architects
594 Braodway, Suite 1204
New York, NY 10012
Phone: (212) 334-9350
Fax: (212) 334-9009
www.asfourguzy.com

Stone Barns Center for Food and Agriculture
630 Bedford Road
Pocantico Hills, NY 10591
Phone: (914) 366-6200
www.stonebarnscenter.org
Designer:
Machado and Silvetti Associates
560 Harrison Avenue, Third Floor
Boston, MA 02118
Phone: (617) 426-7070
Fax: (617) 426-3604
www.machado-silvetti.com

Okada Wynn Las Vegas
3131 Las Vegas Blvd South
Las Vegas, NV 89109
Phone: 1-888-352-DINE
www.wynnlasvegas.com
Designer:
Hirsch Bedner Associates
3216 Nebraska Avenue
Santa Monica, CA 90404
Phone: (310) 829-9087
Fax: (310) 453-1182
www.hbadesign.com

Solea
W Hotel Mexico City
Campos Eliseos 252
Mexico City, Mexico 9138 1818
Phone: 525 5 91 381 1818
www.soleamexico.com
Designer:
Studio GAIA
401 Washington St., Fourth Floor
New York, NY 10013
Phone: (212) 680-3500
Fax: (212) 680-3535
www.studiogaia.com

Nobu 57
40 West 57th Street
New York, NY 10019
Phone: (212) 757-3000
www.noburestaurants.com
Designer:
The Rockwell Group
5 Union Square West
New York, New York 10003
Phone: (212) 463-0335
www.rockwellgroup.com